9 MONEY MISTAKES DOCTORS MAKE

9 MONEY MISTAKES DOCTORS MAKE

and How You, Doctor, Can Avoid Losing Literally Millions of Dollars

VICKI RACKNER, MD, FACS

THRIVING DOCTORS

9 MONEY MISTAKES DOCTORS MAKE: AND HOW YOU, DOCTOR, CAN AVOID LOSING LITERALLY MILLIONS OF DOLLARS

ISBN: 978-1-947557-15-4

Library of Congress data on file with the publisher

Production and publishing services by Concierge Marketing Inc.

Printed in the United States of America

10 9 8 7 6 5 4 3 2

CONTENTS

INTRODUCTION

Dale, a neurosurgeon in his late fifties, said, "I just don't understand it. I make more in a year than my parents made in their working lifetimes. Now my retired parents are living the dream. I, on the other hand, wonder if I will ever be able to retire. How could I be so successful as a physician but make such a mess of money?"

Every day I hear the financial stories of highly respected physicians and dentists. Some have the financial freedom to do what they want to do when they want to do it. Marci, a pediatrician, could have retired at fifty. She continues seeing patients because it's work she loves. Physicians like Marci have control over their money.

The majority of doctors are not as financially secure as they would like to be. Justin said, "I just let money slip through my fingers. I look back with regrets." Linda said, "If I could only have a financial do-over!" As they tell their stories, the phrase, "If only I had avoided…" came up again and again.

The goal of this book is to help you avoid the number-one killer of doctors' hopes and dreams: threats to your financial security.

This focus aligns with Warren Buffett's wealth-building advice. He has two investing rules, and here they are:

Rule #1: Avoid losses.

Rule #2: Don't forget rule #1.

Here you'll learn how to avoid the nine most common ways physicians and dentists let literally millions of dollars slip through their fingers.

When you combine your high earning potential with the commitment to avoid costly mistakes, you are in an excellent position to build wealth.

Why is the conversation about money so critical?

As you think about how to design your career and your life, money buys choices. Financial security gives you options about how long you continue to see patients, indulge a passion, or create an endowment. It gives you the freedom to put your family first or take a business risk.

Conversely financial insecurity limits choices. I met a physician who had a vision for a holistic integrative weight loss clinic. But she could not move forward because she was living paycheck to paycheck.

The reason to build wealth is to have the freedom to do what you want to do when you want to do it. Wealth helps you design a career and life that bring you satisfaction. I call it "living in your sweet spot."

Why are conversations about money so difficult for physicians and dentists?

Conversations about money are difficult because money is the ultimate taboo topic for doctors.

In the world of business, money is the metric by which success is measured. Business people invest in skills to help them build and grow money. They take pride in their profitability and announce it to their shareholders.

We doctors, on the other hand, use patient outcomes to measure our professional success. Never in our training did most of us get any information about how to build wealth or run a profitable organization. In fact, for many doctors, wealth is a four-letter word.

While managing finances is outside of our day-to-day experience, we are skilled at assessing and treating disease. So let us call on our medical knowledge to understand finances.

Financial health/disease mirrors cardiovascular health/disease.

- Just as oxygen fuels cells, money fuels lives. When demand outstrips supply, there's pain.

- There is a spectrum of health and disease. You can be anywhere on the financial health spectrum between wealth— the financial freedom to do what you want to do when you want to do it—and bankruptcy.

- In a mild form of financial insufficiency, you only feel the pain under exertion, like when you're paying for college for three kids when a fourth announces her engagement. As insufficiency progresses, financial worries may wake you up at night. Late-stage financial disease erodes joy and contributes to the epidemic of burnout.

- Financial disease can be embarrassing. In early stages of financial disease, you may feel social embarrassment about not being able to enjoy the lifestyle you expected. Financial professionals use the term financial embarrassment—the condition in which the lack of money causes problems. In late stages of financial disease, you might experience the medical interpretation of the word embarrassment as in "cardiac embarrassment." You find it difficult to function as a result of the disease.

- Known risk factors contribute to disease. Replace smoking, a sedentary lifestyle, and hypertension with overspending, procrastination, and a vulnerability to investing in Dumb Doctor Deals (explained later in this book), and you see the parallel.

- Knowledge is not enough to prevent and treat disease. People generally don't develop heart disease because they lack knowledge; they develop heart disease because of the difficulty in making healthy moment-to-moment choices. Most people know how to build wealth: Spend less than you earn. Start saving and invest early. Don't lose money. Easier said than done!

- We are resilient. We can recover from financial setbacks just like we can recover from a heart attack.

Sometimes Bad Knowledge Is the Problem

Fifty years ago, my mother's doctor gave her a prescription to help her lose weight and relieve her back pain: start smoking. Now that physicians know the health impacts of tobacco, they make different recommendations.

There are things you think you know about building wealth. What if some of those so-called facts were wrong? What if you didn't know what you didn't know? How soon would you like to know?

Three Financial Truths

Consider these three financial truths:

Truth #1: High incomes do not protect you from financial pain.

We physicians have the opportunity to earn millions of dollars over our medical careers doing work that we love. But income isn't the whole financial story. The ability to build wealth is about a relationship among earning, saving, and investing.

When you manage an ICU patient, for example, you look at the I's and O's. A singular focus on income when building wealth is like a singular focus on input when managing an ICU patient; it's an incomplete picture.

You might have read about Oseola McCarty. Oseola worked as a washerwoman for seventy-five years, saving every penny she could. After her death she left a trust of $150,000 for scholarships.

On the other hand, you can outspend your income, no matter how much you earn.

Financial Reality for Doctors Today

- According to the US Department of Labor Statistics, nine out of the ten top earners in the US call themselves "doctor."

- Half of physicians say they are behind in retirement planning.

- Financial concerns contribute to the epidemic of physician burnout.

- The AMA convened a task force to assess competency in older physicians. Why? Many physicians were working well into retirement years out of need.

- Very few physicians will translate their high incomes into true financial freedom.

Truth #2: Physicians are not immune from outside economic and social forces.

You participate in a global, national, regional, and local economy. The financial health of institutions and people around you contributes to your own financial health in many different ways.

- Consider how your own personal net worth is tied to the performance of the stock market and real estate prices.

- Consider how your patients' personal finances impact their choices about when they seek medical care, whether they take medication as prescribed, or how long it takes them to pay their medical bills.

- Consider how the security of your income is tied to the financial health of the organization in which you practice medicine.

Consider how the financial hardships of aging parents, an alcoholic sibling, or a brother-in-law getting back on his financial feet after his business failed impacts you. Chances are you will feel compelled to help, and this offer comes with consequences.

A decade after the global financial meltdown we are still in the recovery phase. Every year since 2013, the Federal Reserve Board issues a report on the economic health of US households. In the 2017 survey, four in ten adults said that if faced with an unexpected expense of $400, they would either not be able to cover it or would cover it by selling something or borrowing money.

This past year the Feds started collecting data on opioid use in this survey. Could people be turning to opioid use to mask financial pain?

Further, we live in a culture of consumption. We are bombarded with messages that self-worth is tied to the things we buy. This drives the overspending that is the major risk factor for financial insufficiency.

These forces are even stronger for physicians, as we are subject to the "standard of care conundrum." We are taught to systematically observe the clinical practices of physicians in our communities and uphold the standards of care. While these medical standards guide clinical choices, we also observe the cars in the doctors' parking garage, the private schools to which colleagues send their kids, and the size of their vacation homes. Keeping up with the Dr. Joneses is in a sense woven into the fabric of medicine and dentistry.

Warning: Many People Live Financial Lies

Experience has taught me that you cannot assess a person's financial health by looking at their level of consumption. Many people are living a financial lie.

Last, we are becoming increasingly impatient. Attention spans are shorter than ever. We want what we want and we want it NOW. Think about how annoyed you are when a web page does not load immediately, or your text is not returned in 30 nanoseconds.

Wealth-building involves giving up something today for a better tomorrow. The current cultural expectation of immediate gratification makes it even harder.

Truth #3: Biology impacts behavior.

We would like to think we all make considered, rational choices that promote our enlightened self-interests.

It appears that biological forces that have kept our species alive shape our behavior in ways that undermine our best intentions. The part of our brain activated when tempted by a second piece of chocolate cake has a difficult time connecting today's actions—spending or saving—and tomorrow's consequences.

Humans have triggers for behaviors, but we fail to plan for them.

People who go through rehab are advised to avoid people and places associated with the substances they abused. They avoid the triggers that increase the risk of recurrence.

Triggers for spending lurk in your blind spot. Knowing what they are and how to avoid them can promote your financial health.

Saving is a habit of wealth. It's also hard! You can make it much easier when you automate it, so that you never see the money that is getting saved.

Part of building wealth is managing the challenge of connecting our current behaviors with future consequences. This brain wiring just isn't there for some people.

We fail to have a healthy respect for the challenge of change. If you want to transform the state of physical or financial health, you have to make different choices. Change is not easy; we fight our biology in order to make changes, even when the current reality makes us miserable. Women will leave abusive partners, for example, six times before they leave for good.

Steve Martin Talks Money

Have you ever heard comic Steve Martin tell audiences, "You can be a millionaire...and never pay taxes! You say, 'Steve, how can I be a millionaire and never pay taxes? First, get a million dollars. Then when the tax man comes knocking at your door and asks why you haven't paid taxes, you say, 'I forgot.'"

My Story

I spend my days helping physicians design careers and lives that work for them. Again and again I saw that past financial mistakes limited their personal and professional options. Many of these physicians thought they were alone in making these mistakes. Because of their money shame, they suffered in silence.

It's time to break the silence!

In the spirit of full disclosure, I am not a financial advisor. I neither sell financial products nor promote an investing philosophy. In fact, I have no formal training or expertise in money management.

My main qualifications for writing this book are this: I've listened to the stories of hundreds of physicians and observed trends. I've also made almost every financial mistake I write about.

Please do not read this book for specific financial advice; read this book to make a list of topics you discuss with members of your financial dream team.

I want to help you avoid the obvious and costly mistakes I see smart, successful physicians make. Here is my story.

I remember it like it was yesterday. In a quiet moment between patients—and there were lots of them in the months after I completed my surgical residency and launched my own private practice—I sat at my desk enjoying the summer sun as it bathed my face.

Suddenly I felt a jolt of cold fear run through my body. Some women have hot flashes. I was experiencing what I came to recognize as a flash of money worries.

I worried about the immediate future. Would I be able to meet my payroll this month? How long would it be until my income was in the same ballpark as the average general surgeon? How in the world was I going to pay back my $100,000 medical school debt?

I contemplated my financial future. In the next few years, what standard of living would my family enjoy? I also knew that one day I would want to retire, but that seemed so far away it was hard to even contemplate.

Looking at the cars in the physicians' parking lot, I had the impression that everyone had made it. When would my husband and I be a two-Porsche family?

I loved taking care of patients. I hated worrying about money. What I most wanted was to get to the point in which I felt in control of my money—rather than having money have control over me.

The problem was that I neither had the financial literacy nor the financial plan to get to financial independence.

Over time I came to understand that I was not alone in my money worries. Some of those physician Porsche owners were also concerned about money. In fact, often the physicians who purchased the trappings of wealth were experiencing the biggest financial pressures.

Exploring physicians and their relationship with money became a passion of mine. I've listened to the financial stories of hundreds of physicians and dentists. I've asked myself, "What separates struggling physicians from thriving physicians?" The trends I identified are in my book The Myth of the Rich Doctor. I encourage you to read that next.

But, here, in this book I want to help you avoid the common costly financial mistakes that set physicians back. I set forth nine of them.

How This Book Is Organized

As I reflected on my conversations with physicians, dentists, and business people, a trend became clear. Quite simply, successful people avoid costly mistakes better than struggling people. Further, they have built systems to minimize their losses when luck is not on their side.

Three categories of mistakes emerged:

- Failure to embrace habits of wealth: The wealthy know how to put their money to work making money.

- Failure to embrace sound business practices: The wealthy know how to optimize their income potential.

- Failure to plan for costly and improbable disasters: The wealthy know how to avoid and bounce back from adversity.

These are the three sections of the book. I offer my insights in hopes that this knowledge will help you do the following:

- Avoid letting millions of dollars slip through your fingers.

- Avoid regrets.

- Treat yourself with more compassion as you understand why you made the choices you have in the past.

- Form healthier financial habits.

- Help your patients get better medical outcomes as you bring some of these ideas about how to make choices that lead in the direction of health to the practice of medicine.

Let's learn from other doctors who have made mistakes with money and see if applying some of the powerful principles in this book will help you live your dreams.

PART I
FAILURE TO EXECUTE
HABITS OF WEALTH

MISTAKE #1: FAILURE TO PLAN FOR THE BIOLOGY OF BEHAVIOR

Key Ideas

- Your financial habits shape your financial destiny.
- Managing your money begins with managing yourself.
- Managing yourself is harder than you might think.

The past president of the American Heart Association was a guest on a national news show to discuss what's new in heart disease. This cardiologist started with the good news: Treatment of cardiovascular disease is highly effective.

Then he delivered the bad news: The incidence of heart disease is increasing. The cost of treatment doubled from $200 billion to $400 billion in the decade that preceded the interview. He concluded that if we do not make a transition to promoting heart health, treatment of this disease will bankrupt us.

The interviewer asked, "Why is treatment so expensive?" The cardiologist pointed out that two thirds of that cost is associated with hospital care for treatment of a heart attack. Yet, a year after the acute cardiac event, only 40% of patients are taking the prescribed three daily medications. The 60% of patients who don't take their medications or fail to take care of themselves come back to the hospital with their next heart attack.

The interviewer ended the interview with this question: "What's the one question you want to see answered?" This distinguished cardiologist opined that we need to solve the behavioral question of how to inspire people to do the things they know they should do to keep themselves healthy.

This chapter is about how to avoid the mistakes that keep you from doing the things you know you should do to build wealth. But this chapter is not as much about money as it is about the biology of behavior. You will take away some ideas from the evolving field of behavioral finance that explain how your own thoughts, feelings, and habits around money contribute to your financial destiny.

Is this a fluff chapter? Consider this: In both 2002 and 2017, the Nobel Prize in economics was awarded to researchers for their contributions to behavioral economics. This may well be the most important chapter in this book.

Further, I hope some of the ideas in this chapter can help you increase compliance among your patients!

Biology vs Wealth-Building

Wealth-building is not rocket science. Save. Start early. Invest wisely.

Why, then, are half of doctors behind in retirement planning?

Being human poses a barrier to building wealth. Please allow that thought to sink in for a minute. The nature of the human condition makes it hard to act in a way that leads to wealth. We behave in predictably irrational ways.

If you manage your money by acting on your biological urges day after day, you will not build wealth. In fact, this is how people go broke.

Your financial habits—the balance between your spending and your saving, as well as the risk you assume when investing—determine the rate at which you build wealth.

Failure to recognize and plan for the biological forces that shape behavior represents a barrier to building wealth.

Here are a few tidbits about what we know about the intersection between biology and wealth:

- **Born spenders and savers.** When you decide about whether to purchase something you want, the nucleus accumbens—a portion of the brain involved in reward and addiction—lights up. Conversely when you are concerned about the cost, the insula—a part of the brain that activates in times of fear—lights up. Neurologists suggest that spenders and savers are wired to be more sensitive to one part of the brain than another, much like being biologically programmed to be right-handed or left-handed.

- **Born risk takers.** Studies of skiers and snowboarders show that those willing to take more risks on the mountain had specific variations of the DRD4 gene. The propensity to assume risk has clear financial consequences.

- **Illness and financial choices.** Overspending seen during episodes of mania, compulsive gambling, and dementia lead to devastating consequences.

When research subjects are put in functional MRIs and asked to make choices, it's not the cerebral cortex that usually lights up; it's the limbic system.

In other words, emotion drives motion. The limbic system does not connect today's choices with tomorrow's consequences. Our animal instincts are all about the here and now.

You may do some research before you buy your next car; however, when you arrive at the dealership, the salesperson's comment, "You look great behind the wheel of that car!" can lead you to make an impulse purchase.

Have you ever felt the inner conflict when your feeling brain says, "You deserve a treat; buy it!" and your thinking brain says, "Let's save this to build wealth more quickly"? Usually the emotional brain wins.

Squirreling Away Resources

Squirrels do not need to be taught to stash acorns for the winter. Their biology leads to the behavior of "scatter hoarding" or "larder hoarding." Foxes, moles, and mice also save for the winter.

Unfortunately, we are not one species biologically programmed for saving.

Humans and Monkeys

Laurie Santos, a professor of psychology at Yale, studies the "spending and saving" behaviors of monkeys. She begins by teaching the monkeys how to trade tokens for food "sold" by human vendors. Then she teaches the monkeys that different vendors offer different value. One vendor may exchange a single grape for a token, while another exchanges two grapes for a token.

Santos finds that the monkeys prefer the vendor who delivers the highest value. Further, monkeys don't save. They often steal from one another and from the vendor.

What if we humans were subject to similar biologic forces as these monkeys?

Our thinking brains know that we can and should be different than the monkeys by saving more and spending less; however, the emotional brain—not the thinking brain—makes the bulk of the day-to-day financial choices.

How Biology Leads to Costly Financial Choices

Here's how your biology undermines your efforts to build wealth:

Immediate gratification. We live in a time of immediate gratification. "Buy now and pay later" has become a national anthem as well as an advertising slogan.

I am a passionate gardener, and I love to buy plants. That's my version of the story. My son tells a different story: "Mom, you're like a crack addict when it comes to plants. You just keep buying and buying." He now refers to nurseries as my "crack houses" and recommends I just stay away.

Buying plants feels good right now. Spending elicits a release of dopamine. Still, my son has a good point.

Procrastination. The easiest way to build wealth is to save and invest early and let the power of compound interest over time do its magic. Compound interest is often called the eighth wonder of the world. You will learn more about this in the next chapter.

Now consider this. Imagine your freshman college roommate was a computer science major and went to work for Microsoft right after completing his undergraduate degree. Further, he started saving 10% out of every paycheck.

You, on the other hand, made different choices. Instead of saving and investing at age twenty-one, you took out loans to attend medical school. This is a prudent financial choice that left you with a different financial reality than your college buddy. First, you're on the losing side of compound interest as you manage your student loans. Second, you lost about a decade of earning during your training, and you launched your career with debt.

You made an investment for your career as a physician or dentist. This is a prudent investment, even though this career choice robs you of the wealth-building power of a decade of time and compound interest.

Here's where biology makes things worse. After all the years of deprivation, you tell yourself, "My family and I deserve nice things now that I'm making some money." The desire for immediate gratification—even though your gratification has been put on hold for many, many years—puts you even further behind.

Burnout and Spending

I was at a medical meeting delivering my talk The Myth of the Rich Doctor. I stayed to listen to the next speaker: a Harvard psychiatrist who spoke about burnout. He talked about the evidence that excessive stress is toxic to the brain, and one of the vulnerable spots was the nucleus accumbens. This is the same portion of the brain activated in pleasurable spending. Could this be the biological answer that helps explain why many stressed people find that "retail therapy" is therapeutic?

How Biology Leads to Costly Investing Mistakes

Economists Daniel Kahneman and Richard Thaler, both winners of the Nobel Prize in economics, know that investors behave irrationally.

For years, economists made projections based on models in which ideal investors made logical choices that promoted their highest self-interest. They could change the variables, like tax rates and project what would happen.

Kahneman asked whether he could take the model and retrospectively predict the tech boom and bust. He could not. It was only when he paid attention to the actual observed behaviors of the real live investors that things made sense.

Real investors made different choices than ideal investors. Kahneman wondered if there was a way to understand, explain, and predict what appear to be the irrational investing choices of the real investors.

Here are some of the predictable investing errors Kahneman describes are these:

- **Loss aversion.** We will take greater risks to avoid loss than to experience gains. We hang onto stocks as their value falls because we hate to sell at a loss; hanging onto the stock usually results in even greater losses. Investors predictably take risks at the time they should be erring on the side of safety.

- **Over- and underreactions.** Investors tend to behave with optimism when the market goes up, and become much more pessimistic when the market goes down.

- **Overconfidence.** Investors tend to overestimate their ability to beat the market and underestimate investing challenges.

- **Relativity.** Investors see the world through the eyes of relative experience. Imagine how you would feel if someone gave you a gift card. Now imagine how you would respond if someone gave you two gift cards and took one back. You have the identical outcome in each case, but it feels much different.

Part of the human condition is the propensity to let emotion drive investing choices. This usually results in costly errors as investors buy and sell at the wrong time and fail to recognize the real investment risk.

A physician said, "The main thing my financial advisor does is protect me from myself!"

Your Childhood Lessons about Money Matter

Alex is a highly respected clinician who attracts patients from a five-state area. This leaves her life partner wondering why she makes such irrational choices about money.

Through their disciplined approach to saving and investing, this couple built an investment portfolio worth about $9 million. Still, Alex refused to spend money. They had staycations instead of the international travel Alex's colleagues enjoyed. They drove ten-year-old cars. When the refrigerator finally died, Alex rejected the idea of upgrading their kitchen with stainless steel kitchen appliances, even though they both enjoyed cooking.

Alex's partner said to me, "Alex has a fear of being a bag lady one day. On some level she knows this fear is irrational; sometimes I remind her that even if we tried, we would not be able to spend $9 million in our lives. Still she carries around this money fear all the time. She's in private practice, and if she has a low patient load in any given week or month, she gets frantic because of the loss of income. I wish we could avoid the regular fights we have about money."

Why does Alex—a physician with excellent clinical judgment—make spending choices that defy logic?

The clues are in her childhood. Alex grew up in a series of foster homes, and money was always tight. As she thinks about her kitchen remodel, she is not responding to today's financial reality; she is responding as the nine-year-old who worried about whether she would get enough to eat. Alex suffers from financial PTSD.

Children have a biological propensity to grow into adults who recreate their parents' financial reality, with or without childhood financial trauma. They absorb their parents' beliefs about the meaning of money and the ways in which money works.

It does not have to be this way.

Jenifer said, "I watched my parents struggle with money. It's like they had holes in their pockets, spending every penny they got. In high school, I got tired of having our power turned off, so I got a job and paid the electric bill myself. I vowed I would learn how to manage money and build wealth." And she has! She practices in an office building she owns and bought a home for her mother.

Alex's dysfunctional childhood lessons about money helped her accumulate wealth, but prevents her from enjoying it.

Jenifer could have followed in her parents' dysfunctional financial footsteps. It's easy to spend more than you earn. However, she got the help she needed to create a different financial reality for herself.

If you see yourself or others making irrational money choices, consider whether childhood money lessons could be part of the problem.

You Feel Worthy of Wealth?

Many physicians express mixed feelings about building wealth. One doctor said, "Wealth feels like a four-letter word." One one hand, they want the freedom and security that wealth brings; on the other hand, they have difficulties reconciling their commitment to service with the reality that those services generate profit.

Your financial health impacts every part of your personal and professional life. Here are some reasons to build wealth:

- **Financial security opens doors to professional possibilities.** Wealth gives you more choices as you consider how you position yourself for success in the political climate of dramatic change.

- **Financial security helps you avoid distracted doctoring.** Money worries serve as a constant source of distraction. Just as you wouldn't text and drive, similarly, you should avoid distractions when treating patients.

- **Financial security helps you put your family's needs first.** A colleague decided to cut back on her ER shifts when her children became adolescents. She knew she wanted to be there to guide her kids through that tricky stage of development. She also knew that she could afford it.

- **Financial security immunizes you from burnout.** Insufficient income is one of the top risk factors for developing burnout. Further, insufficient savings and debt correlate with burnout.

- **Financial security helps you treat burnout.** You may decide to cut back on your hours, create a specialty focus in your practice, or launch an entrepreneurial venture like writing a blog or building a company around a medical invention you made.

- **Financial security helps you put the patients' needs first.** You may remember the case of the Michigan oncologist who was found guilty of a $35 million Medicare fraud scheme. This doctor harmed, and in some cases killed, his patients by administering chemotherapy that the patients did not need for his own financial gain. I remember the hushed whispers about the orthopedic surgeon who was performing surgical procedures that were only marginally indicated because he needed the income.

- **Financial security helps you leave a legacy and serve in a bigger way.** The greater your wealth, the greater impact you can make for your family and for worthy causes you're passionate about.

Just Do It

If you have been procrastinating with your savings, don't beat yourself up. Just do it! They say the best time to plant a tree is twenty years ago. The second best time is today.

Decide Who's the Boss—You or Your Emotions

Have you ever known a family in which the children run the house? The parents will do anything the kids want because the core family value, I guess, is keeping the kids happy.

Letting your emotions determine your choices is like asking your kids to assume family leadership.

One of the most important interventions for building wealth is moving beyond your biology and making choices that are divorced from emotion. Make your financial choices in your thinking brain—not your feeling brain. In other words, set up systems that will make it easier to take the actions that help you build wealth.

You will have emotions that will stir up impulses and longing. That's okay. You can just observe them. Don't let your emotions control you and your choices. Stay in control of your actions, regardless of what you are feeling. You don't have to feel like doing the right thing to do it.

The Challenge of Change

A *New York Times* best-selling author tells me why she has the same meal every Monday night, saying, "I get paid to imagine things. Since I can only imagine so many things, I don't want to waste my efforts imagining what I'll cook for dinner on Monday night."

Our brains are wired to put activities on auto-pilot so we can attend to novelty in the environment. Think about how hard you had to concentrate to make a left turn when you were learning how to drive. Now you can easily drive to your office while listening to the radio or considering the patient in the ER you are driving to see.

Your habits shape health outcomes. The habit of eating healthy foods supports weight loss. Just as regular exercise promotes cardiac health, the habit of regularly saving 10% of your income supports financial health.

Conversely, unhealthy habits erode financial health. To promote health, you want to replace unhealthy habits with healthy habits.

Here's the problem. Replacing unhealthy habits with healthy habits is no easy task. How many times have you ever kept a New Year's resolution?

Here are some ideas about how to make changes a little less painful:

- **Have a vision of your goal.** If, for example, you want to increase your savings rate, imagine what it will feel like when work is optional. Make it a multisensory vision and live in your thoughts when the going gets tough.

- **Don't rely on willpower.** This is a limited resource.

- **Understand the triggers for bad choices.** I, for example, decided to shop at a different grocery store so I didn't drive by my favorite nursery when I went to buy cat food.

- **Create a system that makes it easier to change.** Automate savings by having the amount automatically transferred into a brokerage account. Create a family rule that you will not spend over a certain amount before checking with others. Make a public commitment. Then let members of your community help hold you accountable.

- **Know where each penny goes.** I joined my son's powerlifting team celebration after a meet. I sat next to a powerlifter who is a retired state supreme court justice. At the end of the meal, she took out a pocket notebook and started writing. I asked what she was doing, and she told me she kept track of every penny she spent. She said she started doing this because she had no idea where her money went. She found, however, that the simple act of recording her spending changed her spending in healthy ways.

- **Understand who influences your choices.** You have read about mirror neurons. We are literally wired to connect and fit in. Online retailers like Amazon know the choices of people who are like you and who will influence the choices you make; that's why ratings are so important. Choose your friends wisely. Understand that you will want to do what they do.

- **Know that change is possible.** I have personally seen physicians and dentists who transformed their financial lives. No matter where you are today, there's a more hopeful tomorrow.

Your Biology Is Not Your Destiny

Your biology does not condemn you to making these predictable wealth-building errors. You can find ways to manage yourself—your own thoughts, feelings, and actions around money—to promote your financial health.

You may not be able to change the circuitry in your brain. I know that I will never get rid of my urge to stop at nurseries and go on spending sprees. Yet I do now this: The more insight I have about my brain wiring, the more likely I am to make better choices. The more I can simply be a witness to the choices I make, the more likely I am to have control over those urges.

Action Steps

- Ask your financial advisor to project your financial future if you maintain your current habits of saving, spending, and investing.

- If your current financial habits are not helping you get to the financial finish line as quickly as you would like, explore ways to tweak your financial habits.

Consider these questions:

- What are your triggers for spending?

- What systems can you put in place to spend less and save more?

- What systems can you put in place to remove emotion from investing choices?

MISTAKE #2: FAILURE TO HARNESS THE POWER OF LEVERAGE

Key Ideas

- Leverage allows you to do more with less.
- You can leverage other people's money, time, work, and wisdom.
- Leverage the power of compound interest over time.

Francis and Glynis practically grew up together. They both went to medical school, and both became cardiologists. Both earned handsome incomes. Both were still paying off medical school debt.

Francis learned that Glynis purchased an apartment building. She asked her friend, "How did you do that?" Her friend offered a one-word answer, "Leverage."

What Is Leverage?

Leverage is the power to do more with less.

Think about using an Allen wrench. You can put the long end of the wrench into the screw, or the short end. If you put the short end in, you have a longer lever arm and exert less force to get the job done. This is the power of leverage.

Archimedes said, "Give me a lever and I can move the world."

Your efforts to build wealth do not have to be limited by the number of hours you work in a day, the amount of money you have to invest, or the limitations of your knowledge and experience. You can leverage the resources of others to accelerate your progress toward wealth.

The wealthy harness the power of leverage. You can too. In fact, the failure to harness the power of leverage could cost you millions of dollars. Here are some forms of leverage:

1. Other People's Money

You've heard the adage "It takes money to make money." However, it doesn't need to be your money. The use of other people's money can accelerate your progress toward financial freedom.

Let's say you want to buy a new house. You could sell some stocks and bonds that are earning about 6% and purchase the house for cash. Should you do that—or take out a 3% mortgage?

While there are emotional benefits to owning your home outright, there are financial benefits to carrying a mortgage beyond the tax deduction. If you could borrow money at 3% to invest in a low-risk asset that generates 6%, you would do that all day long!

The wealthy have a term for putting other people's money to work making money; it's called gearing. Just like your bike can go faster in the right gear, so, too, you can gear up the purchases of assets by using other people's money.

Real estate developers are known for their habits of borrowing money to invest in the project. They know that they will be profitable even after they have paid the interest on the loan. The great irony, of course, is that the less you need the loan, the more likely you are to get it.

Factor in the power of leverage as you make choices about how you pay back your student loans.

2. Other People's Time

You can hire others to do tasks that you could theoretically do, such as cleaning your house, maintaining your yard, and building a deck. Having other people do work allows you to invest your time, instead, in the activities that bring you the greatest rewards.

3. Other People's Work

You can hire people to optimize the profitability of your practice. This may involve office staff, a physician partner, physician assistants, dental techs, or nurse practitioners. The amount of leverage you get is the difference between the net revenue that they generate and the expense of hiring them.

4. Other People's Experience and Expertise

You could potentially file your own taxes, create your own will, or even represent yourself in court. Yet this approach is often penny wise and pound foolish. You have the greatest leverage when you call on the experience of the experts and get things done right.

This quote has been credited to Rita Mae Brown and others, and it makes sense: "Good judgment comes from experience, and experience comes from poor judgment."

5. Compound Interest Plus Time

Compound interest has been described as the eighth wonder of the world. Owning an asset that compounds is like owning the goose that lays the golden eggs. Over time, you'll collect the golden eggs. And more golden geese can hatch from some of these golden eggs. The longer you hang onto the goose, the more golden eggs you will collect.

When you sell an asset, you lose the goose and the golden eggs it would have laid.

Selling an asset to buy a better asset makes financial sense; however, selling an asset to take a dream vacation can be very costly.

Like the example of the washerwoman earlier in the book, time—a key part of the compounding equation—helped Oseola McCarty turn her meager early earnings and small investments into hundreds of thousands of dollars.

Be on the Right Side of Compound Interest

Pay off high-interest compounding loans. You don't want your lender to be the beneficiary of the magic of compound interest.

With leverage, you're not alone. You can tap the strengths of all the resources you need around you. Leverage is essential to create wealth. Those who become wealthy understand, master, and fully utilize leverage.

Action Steps

Consider these questions:

- How can you harness the power of leverage to build wealth more effectively?

- Does your plan for paying off debt—whether it's your student loans, credit cards, or mortgage—make financial sense?

- How can you leverage the work and expertise of others to free up time or generate more revenue?

MISTAKE #3:
FAILURE TO MANAGE TAXES

Key Ideas

- Taxes represent your biggest lifetime expense.
- Most high-earning physicians and dentists will see their taxes rise under the new tax law.
- Consult with a tax strategist to make the new tax law work for you.

After a long career as an oncologist, John was ready to spend some serious time on the golf course. He was on the fourth hole when he got a call from his CPA. "I have some bad news. You know that blue chip stock that you inherited from your mother and sold this year to buy your vacation home? The IRS just sent you a bill for about $50,000."

Why You Need to Pay Attention to Taxes

Sophisticated investors understand that proactively managing taxes is one of the most effective strategies for building wealth. Why? Taxes represent your biggest lifetime expense.

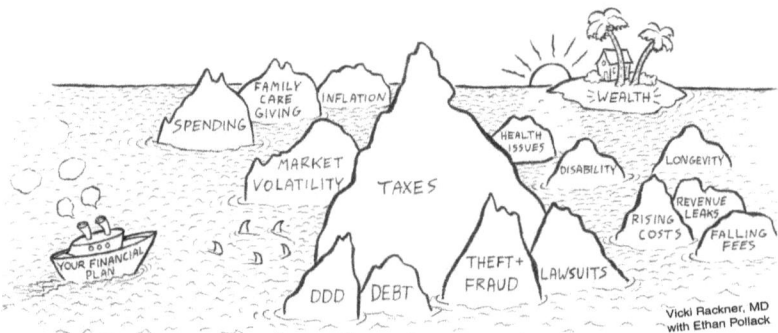

Vicki Rackner, MD
with Ethan Pollack

The way you manage your lifetime tax burdens impacts the rate at which you build wealth.

Let's say, for example, you want to move up your retirement date by five to ten years. You have three basic choices:

1. Increase your income.

2. Get better returns on your investments.

3. Cut your costs.

What single intervention will have the biggest impact—at the lowest risk? It's cutting your costs by cutting your taxes.

Every dollar you keep instead of paying to Uncle Sam is a dollar that you can put to work growing your wealth. Conversely, without proactive management, taxes will erode your wealth and the legacy you pass on to the next generations.

Here are some important things to understand about taxes.

Taxes Are a Form of Social Engineering

Tax law is a form of social engineering, designed to reward specific behaviors that benefit society at large. Saving for retirement, making long-term investments, creating jobs, building houses, and giving to worthy causes all are rewarded with reduced tax burdens.

When you align your investing choices with the rewarded behaviors, you build wealth more effectively.

How the Tax Law and Jobs Act Impacts You

As you know, in 2017 a new tax code became law. This is the most sweeping tax reform in over thirty years. The goal of the new tax law is to strengthen the US economy by making us more competitive in a global market. The old corporate tax rate of up to 35% was one of the highest in the world. Logic suggests that if we lowered the corporate tax rate, we could attract more business and investments here. This idea has bipartisan support.

Tax breaks only for the wealthy would be politically untenable. To pass, the new tax law also included tax benefits for the employees of these corporations. Further, reducing corporate tax rates without reducing the taxes of small business owners would make passage of the new law difficult.

How would the government make up the revenue lost through these tax cuts to these three groups?

High-earning professionals like you will now shoulder a larger share of taxes.

How? Many deductions you have used to lower your tax bill in the past have been tightened or eliminated, including personal exemptions, state and local taxes, mortgage interest, and many others.

Some doctors ask, "How does the new tax law work?" The better question to ask is, "How can I make the tax law work for me? How can I harness the power of the corporate changes and put them to work for me?"

Isn't that my CPA's job? You might be thinking, "I've got my taxes under control. I work with a CPA who works with lots of doctors." You may be right!

However, the reality is that most CPA's are tax historians. He or she summarizes the financial activities of the calendar year and calculates the taxes you owe. Further, your CPA is only as good as his or her knowledge about tax law, and tax law is complex.

A tax strategist—who may be a CPA, a financial advisor, a tax attorney or combination—can help you proactively make choices that could significantly reduce your tax bill.

For example, I know a tax strategist who just helped a surgeon reduce his tax bill by $948,000 in 2018. Contrast that with the story of a surgeon who planned to fund his retirement through the sale of his stake in a surgical center. Unfortunately, because he did not structure the sale in the right way, the unplanned capital gains taxes derailed his retirement dreams.

How Do Tax Strategists Find Tax Savings?

Tax strategists have four basic tools to reduce your tax bills:

Code-based strategies. The new tax code brings wide-ranging changes. At this moment, sharp minds are hard at work trying to find ways of making the codes work in favor of their tax-paying clients.

Your tax strategists can find ways of making the new tax code work for you. For example, changing your corporate structure or shifting from a W2 employee to a 1099 independent consultant could make a significant difference.

Can your current CPA help you with code-based strategies? Maybe or maybe not.

If your CPA is a true tax strategist, he or she would have called you early in 2018 and said, "The new tax law is a huge opportunity for you. Let's get together and consider some changes we can make early in 2018 to reduce your tax bill."

If your CPA did not make this call to you, I invite you to get a second opinion from a true tax strategist. There is too much money on the line. Please don't leave tax savings on the table!

Is the idea of reducing your taxes legally and ethically by going with the momentum of the tax code unpatriotic? Will you be subject to increased scrutiny? Will you increase your risk for an audit?

Judge Learned Hand said, "There is not even a patriotic duty to increase one's taxes. Over and over again the Courts have said that there is nothing sinister in so arranging affairs as to keep taxes as low as possible. Everyone does it, rich and poor alike and all do right, for nobody owes any public duty to pay more than the law demands."

Timing strategies. Each source of income can be assigned to one of three buckets:

- **Taxable income.** The more you make, the more you're taxed

- **Tax-deferred income.** When you put money in your retirement plan like your 401(k) or IRA, you enjoy a lower taxable income for that year; however you will pay taxes when you withdraw the money at the tax rate in that year.

- **Tax-free income.** Specific sources of income are not taxed. For example, it makes sense that orphans and widows would not pay taxes on life insurance benefits after the death of the breadwinner.

In general, paying taxes later instead of paying now is generally a good idea. However, this strategy comes with the uncertainty. What will the future tax rates be?

Most economists agree that the tax rate you will pay when you withdraw money from your retirement plan will almost certainly be higher than the historically low tax rate you pay today. Further, chances are good that your expenses in retirement will go up—not down.

Income-shifting strategies. You do not have to put all of your income in one bucket. You can potentially create different business entities. This is an approach tax strategists call "cracking and packing." Have you considered shifting income to people like your children who are in lower tax brackets?

Product-based strategies. Just as you have access to new diagnostic and therapeutic tools, so, too, many financial tools can be used to lower your tax burdens, including Employee Stock Ownership Plans (ESOP), Cash Balance Plans (CBP), Charitable Remainder Unit Trusts (CRUT), captive insurance companies and many more.

> ## *Doing Well by Doing Good*
>
> *You can do well by doing good. Structure your charitable donations in a way that makes your contributions go further, allows you to enjoy tax benefits during your life, and preserves your legacy after your death.*

Speak with your own tax strategist about how you can make the tax law work for you. Even if you are happy with your CPA, get a second opinion about your taxes. In this way you can potentially avoid letting millions of dollars in tax savings slip through your fingers.

Action Steps

- Consult with a tax strategist to explore ways to make the new tax law work for you.
- Reassess whether your current plan to defer taxes serves you.
- Explore whether any financial products or services could help you reduce your taxes now, minimize your taxes in retirement, and protect your estate after your death.

PART II
FAILURE TO EMBRACE SOUND BUSINESS PRACTICES

MISTAKE #4: FAILURE TO NEGOTIATE

Key Ideas

- Failure to negotiate can cost you millions of dollars.
- Negotiation is a skill that you can learn and develop.
- Negotiate in the spirit of mutual respect and a sense of fairness.

Hal and Amy completed their orthopedic surgical fellowships at the same time. Hal was offered a position with a starting salary of $450K. Given his $200K medical school debt, this sounded great! He signed the contract.

Amy was offered the same starting salary; however, before signing the contract she successfully negotiated a 10% increase in her starting salary.

Let's say that both remained employees for their thirty-year careers (ages thirty-five to retirement at age sixty-five) and each received a 5% pay raise each year.

Hal will earn $29.9 million during his thirty-year career; Amy will earn $32.9 million. That's a $3 million difference!

Failure to negotiate can be a costly mistake.

You Gain More than Money When You Negotiate

Amy gained more than economic benefits through her willingness to negotiate. A partner later told her, "As Dr. Phil says, 'You teach people how to treat you.' Your willingness to negotiate says, 'I value myself—and I expect you to, too.' You earned my respect."

What Is Negotiation?

Although the idea of negotiating your benefits package may raise your blood pressure, the reality is that you negotiate every day. You negotiate when you inspire patients to take their medication as prescribed, convince your family to go out to your favorite restaurant, or persuade a friend to make a donation to your favorite cause. Negotiation is nothing more than a series of conversations that leads to your getting what you want.

With the financial stakes being so high in specific circumstances—literally measured in millions of dollars, as in my example—why don't more doctors negotiate?

Here are some reasons why only about 10% of physicians negotiate employment contracts:

- **Doctors don't consider the possibility.** In Sheryl Sandberg's book, *Lean In: Women, Work, and the Will to Lead*, she shares that she was a seasoned executive when Mark Zuckerberg invited her to join Facebook as the COO. She says she was inclined to accept the first offer he made. When she discussed it with her husband, he told her the first offer is just the starting point of a negotiation. He recommended she make a counteroffer. She did and Zuckerberg came back to her with a much more lucrative proposal. If Sandberg reached her level of professional success without knowing basic negotiation etiquette, how many physicians make the same mistake?

- **Negotiation makes them feel uncomfortable.** We are not born knowing how to negotiate, and human nature leads us to avoid the things that bring discomfort.

- **Negotiation is not a skill that we are taught in our training.** Negotiation is a skill that can be acquired, yet it's not a formal part of medical school curriculum.

- **Doctors fear losing the offer.** Many physicians and dentists would rather accept the terms offered to them than risk "rocking the boat."

- **Doctors fear they will appear "greedy" or pushy.** You want to be seen as a team player. How can you negotiate and be a team player?

- **Doctors want to avoid conflict.** For many, negotiation smacks of conflict; most doctors would prefer to collaborate than compete.

- **Doctors do not believe in their own value or worthiness.** One of my mentors said, "The first sale is always to yourself."

- **Doctors fear rejection.** Rejection takes many forms from losing a job offer to losing face when a call schedule is not modified as requested.

It should be no surprise, then, that the majority of physicians and dentists do not negotiate—even when we pay the price.

Overcoming the Fear of Rejection

The fear of rejection limited the personal and professional options for Jia Jiang. To overcome his fear, he decided to intentionally create circumstances in which he would be rejected every day for 100 days. He asked a stranger to lend him $100. He asked for a "hamburger refill" at a fast-food restaurant. Experience taught him that the world did not end when someone said, "No." He became less fearful of asking. Invest a few minutes watching his very funny TED talk.

The Negotiating Mindset

Think of negotiation as a mutual process of give and take so each party gets what they want. A divorce mediator said, "I know we have a good settlement when each party is equally unhappy." A successful negotiation leaves each party feeling equally happy.

Negotiate in the spirit of mutual benefit and fairness. Be fair to your negotiation partner. Most importantly, be fair to yourself.

When Should You Negotiate?

Many negotiations have financial impacts. Please consider negotiating under these circumstances:

- Negotiate before you join a new practice.

- Negotiate before you sign a buy-sell agreement.

- Negotiate your professional fees with insurance companies.

- Negotiate the terms of mortgages and other loans.

- Negotiate the interest rates of credit cards.

- Negotiate sale prices of homes and cars.

- Negotiate with patients. Offer a financial incentive for prepayment or early complete payment.

- Negotiate with your phone and internet providers and any vendor that offers a promotional rate (such as subscriptions and travel).

Everything Is Open to Negotiation

Has an insurance company told you they don't negotiate their rates with the contracted providers? That's simply not true. They can and do negotiate. Everything is open to negotiation.

When Should You NOT Negotiate?

I personally do not negotiate professional fees when I hire consultants. I have found that you usually get what you pay for. I vet my lawyers, CPAs, investment advisors, and even real estate agents and choose them because I want the best. I am happy to pay for the value I believe they will add. Further, an attempt to negotiate fees says to your consultant, "I don't value you that much." This is not the way to get optimal performance with them.

Stop negotiating when someone tells you they have made the best offer they can. Circumstances may change in the future, and you could have another chance to negotiate.

What Are Some Negotiation Tips?

- **Do your homework.** If you're negotiating your benefits package, learn the salaries in your medical specialty in that geographic area. If you're negotiating the terms of a loan, know what other lenders charge.

- **Know your negotiation partner.** If a practice or employer is replacing a busy physician who became ill, the practice might be more willing to make concessions to fill the position quickly.

- **Know your bottom line.** Know what you are willing to accept—and what you're unwilling to accept. Always enter into a negotiation with a willingness to walk away.

- **Treat people with respect,** including your negotiation partners and the front office staff.

- **Timing is critical.** Don't begin negotiating too early or too late in the relationship with your negotiating partner. You are in a much better position if your negotiating partner is already "sold" on the value you bring.

- **Be calm.** People can sense fear and desperation. You are in a much better situation to negotiate if you have multiple options.

- **The first sale is to yourself.** In negotiations, you are engaged in an exchange of value. With compensation packages, you are asking a group to pay you for the value of your services. If you don't think you're worth it, they won't either.

- **You don't have to be everyone's friend.** My son is subletting his college apartment because he accepted a summer internship in a different town. A friend of my son referred a friend coming to town for the summer. This person asked for a discount on the rent because he was only going to be there four days a week. While my son wants to be a nice guy and help a friend, his bigger priority is being financially whole. He said, "I understand what you want, but what I want is to have my entire rent covered."

- **Give yourself time.** If a practice makes an offer, you do not have to accept on the spot.

- **Know who is representing whom.** Generally medical recruiters are engaged by the person or organization doing the hiring. It's their duty to represent the best interests of their client—not you.

- **Get creative.** You can exchange value in many different ways. If you're negotiating an employment contract, your potential partners may not be able to increase the base salary, but you could negotiate other benefits such as a moving allowance, paid CME, parking, loans, and tail insurance.

- **Practice, practice, practice.** As with any skill, you will get betterover time.Go to a car dealer and practice your skills without buying, walk away. Learn from the experience.

- **Get it in writing.** Verbal commitments are nice, but remember this piece of wisdom offered by a medical malpractice attorney, "If it isn't in writing, it never happened."

- **Before you sign a contract, seek legal advice.** Attorneys can assure that your best interests are represented and alert you to potential dangers that lurk in the contract.

- **People show you who they are.** Beware of people who are disrespectful of you in the negotiation process or "play unfair." They have shown you who they are. I was hired to write a special report for a colleague whom I believed to be an honorable person. We agreed on the scope of the project and my fee. Normally I do not begin work until my fee is paid, but my colleague expressed urgency, and I thought he was trustworthy so I began writing that day. When the payment did not come, I thought it might be a simple oversight. I sent a few more requests for payment that were ignored. It was only when I told my client I would not continue work that he tried to renegotiate my fee. My grandmother used to say, "Don't believe what people say about themselves; look at what they do."

Strength in Numbers

Why do hospitals negotiate better fees with insurance providers than independent physicians do? It's the power of numbers. Private practice physicians throughout the country have come together to even the playing field by forming independent physician associations or IPAs. An IPA is a legal business entity organized and owned by independent physicians for the purposes of negotiating more favorable contracts.

Who Should Represent You in Negotiations?

Make an investment in basic negotiation skills; this will serve you in all parts of your life. However, know what your negotiation limitations are. Err on the conservative side. If you do not think that you can negotiate a compensation package, hire someone to do it for you.

Have a lawyer review any contract you sign. They may be willing to negotiate for you. Yes, you will pay a fee for this service, but you will almost certainly see a handsome return on this investment. Remember the long-term difference in earnings for the two physicians in my example at the beginning of this chapter.

What Should You Remember?

People with whom you negotiate, including employers, are not engaging in philanthropy; they are conducting business.

Your employer and potential future partner will generate revenue from your clinical activities. They are willing to offer you the salary and benefits package because they will generate profit from the clinical care you deliver.

I have spoken with frustrated physicians who say, "Today there are more and more people generating profits from my efforts."

Keep track of the value you bring. Then think of negotiation as a fair exchange of value.

Action Steps

- Observe how effective you are at getting what you want in your relationships with your colleagues, family, and friends.

- Consider investing in your negotiation skills by reading a book, watching a video, or enrolling in a course.

- Always ask yourself, "Who is the best person to negotiate?"

MISTAKE #5: FAILURE TO OPTIMIZE YOUR EARNING POTENTIAL

Key Ideas

- Your ability to generate revenue is your most valuable asset.
- Your patients, your employer, and potential clients exchange their money for the value you deliver.
- Your value transcends your ability to treat individual patients.

You made a significant investment to enjoy the privilege of caring for patients. You made sacrifices. You work long hours. You deserve to enjoy the fruits of your labors.

Yet many physicians and dentists are leaving money on the exam table. This mistake could cost you millions of dollars over a career.

Different groups of doctors leave money on the exam table for different reasons.

The Most Common Mistakes Employed Doctors Make

Today the majority of physicians are employed. Your ability to negotiate the financial terms of relationships shapes your financial destiny (review the previous chapter about negotiation).

Please remember this: Your employer is running a business. Yes, the hospital or clinic wants to deliver good care, but at the end of the day, they must make a profit to stay in business.

From the perspective of an organization, you are a small profit center. Insurance companies and patients are billed for the care that you deliver. This revenue gets divided and distributed among your salary, the cost of marketing and attracting new patients, the facility overhead, and the handsome salaries of the C-suite executives that lead the organization.

The more revenue you generate for the organization, the higher economic value you bring.

Conversely, the organization is more profitable when they pay their employees less.

The person who cares most about your financial future is YOU. The person who has the greatest power to impact your lifetime earned income is YOU.

Negotiate as You Leave Training and Start Your First Job

Your lifetime income potential is tied to the base salary you accept when you complete your residency for a simple reason: Your raises will be a percentage of your current salary. Negotiating a 10% increase in your starting salary right out of residency or fellowship training could translate to literally millions of dollars in additional earned income over your career.

You can and should get legal counsel before signing your first employment contract. Yes, you will pay a fee for this service; however, you could potentially pay dearly for a failure to negotiate.

Negotiate During Your Performance Reviews

Get some coaching for your performance review to secure a raise that reflects the value you bring. Say, for example, "As you know, I have been delivering talks in the community about Lyme disease. I was just interviewed on the radio and a local paper did an article in which I was quoted. Based on the patient intake information, we know that these efforts attracted at least ten new patients to our clinic this past quarter. After patients see me, they usually transfer their care to our organization, and we know the lifetime value of a new patient to this hospital. In the spirit of fairness, I would like my income to reflect my contributions to the increased profitability of the organization."

This will be an uncomfortable conversation at first. But with coaching and practice, you'll be able to conduct this conversation with greater ease.

The Most Common Mistakes Doctors in Private Practice Make

Success in private practice is contingent on strong clinical skills—and strong business skills. Here are common costly mistakes physicians and dentists in private practice make.

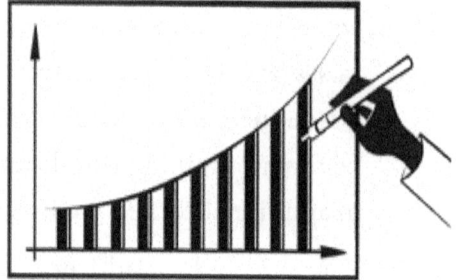

Failure to Know Your Financial Vital Signs

You would never dream of managing a critically ill patient without reviewing the I's and O's. How well do you understand how money flows in and out of your practice? If you're like many busy, successful physicians, you say, "I hire my office manager/CPA to keep track of these things." And that's how it should be.

You want your focus to be on patient care.

No one cares more about your revenue than you do. I highly recommend that you regularly review your financial I's and O's. You can decide how often you want to do it: monthly, quarterly, or semiannually.

Critical data include knowing about

- Your fixed expenses (rent, payroll, insurance, for example)

- Your one-time expenses (CME, equipment purchases)

- Your average accounts receivables

- Your production (how much you bill)

- Write-offs

Failure to Know the Average Revenue of Each Clinical Activity Generates

In the fee-for-service model, you exchange your time for money. Some clinical activities are more profitable than others.

Do you know which diagnostic and procedural codes result in the highest "hourly wage"? Do you have a clear understanding of the range of fees you get from different insurance carriers? Have you considered whether you want to be a participating provider in all of the plans in which you're enrolled?

This kind of information allows you to decide whether you want to attract a certain kind of patient to your practice.

Failure to Collect What You're Owed for Clinical Services

The biggest and costliest mistake I see doctors make is the failure to collect what they are rightfully owed for their clinical services.

Physicians in private practice walk away from an average of 30% of their incomes when they do not follow up on rejected insurance claims. One doctor showed me his "Porsche drawer" filled with rejected claims, saying, "If I only contested these rejections, I could buy my dream car. We're so busy treating patients, though, that we just never seem to find time."

Failure to collect patient copays can be costly too.

The Most Common Mistakes All Doctors Make

Failure to Negotiate Terms of Contracts and Loans

You will most likely borrow money to make big and small purchases. The interest that you pay on a loan is not carved in stone. Shop around. Some banks will match lower interest rates. Call your credit card company and ask them to decrease the interest that you pay.

You are in the best position to negotiate if you have high credit scores.

Being Penny-Wise and Pound-Foolish

You have heard the expression, "You have to spend money to make money."

Sometimes the unwillingness to make investments in yourself can be the costliest income mistakes you will make.

Here are wise ways to spend money that will allow you to increase your income potential.

- **Education and training.** Invest to expand your clinical knowledge, financial literacy, or business skills.

- **Buy more time.** Yes, you can clean your house and mow your lawn. If you find activities like these relaxing, please indulge. But when you hire people to take care of these activities, you buy time to optimize your revenue.

- **Hire experts.** The investment you make seeking expert advice will almost always put you in a better financial position.

- **Buy protection.** Do not skimp on insuring the assets that have the most value to you, including your income potential. It's not a fun or sexy way to spend money, but when you need the protection, you'll be glad you have it.

Failure to Consider a Move

This sounds dramatic. Who would want to uproot their families? There may be personal reasons for moving, such as being closer to aging parents. In addition, there may be a strong financial reason.

Physician compensation is shaped by geographic location. According to the 2016 Medscape Physician Compensation Report, top-earning states include North Dakota, New Hampshire, and Nebraska.

State income tax varies. The amount of money that makes its way into your pocket reflects both your income and your income taxes. Here are some tax facts:

- Seven states do not collect any income taxes: Alaska, Florida, Nevada, South Dakota, Texas, Washington, and Wyoming.

- Two states collect taxes only on dividends and interest income: New Hampshire and Tennessee.

- California has the highest incremental state tax rate: 13.3%.

- Eight states have only one income tax bracket, charging its residents the same rate on all income, which is called a flat rate: Colorado (4.63%), Illinois (3.75%), Indiana (3.3%), Massachusetts (5.10%), Michigan (4.25%), North Carolina (5.75%), Pennsylvania (3.07%), and Utah (5%).

- California also has the largest number of tax brackets (10), ranging from 1% to 13.3%.

The cost of living in a geographic location shapes how far your dollars go. Take a look at real estate, and you will find that you can buy more house in one part of the country than another. The cost of goods and services reflects sales taxes and property taxes.

How much could you improve your financial condition and quality of life with a move? Check with your financial advisor or CPA to run the numbers.

Failure to Explore Sources of Income Not Tied to the Care of Individual Patients

Are you stuck in the belief that the only way you can generate revenue is by treating patients? If so, you could be walking away from many opportunities to generate income and make a difference in the lives of patients, your colleagues, and your community.

A freelance journalist who interviewed me for an article published in the *Wall Street Journal* contacted me when she was hired to write an article about health care consumerism—what patients can do to get better medical care and avoid preventable medical errors. This information was put in front of the millions of readers of this publication. Practicing physicians can help millions of patients with widespread information.

It has been two decades since I earned an income from treating individual patients. I have personally experienced many ways to generate income after hanging up my white coat. Some have been more profitable than others.

My mother was so proud when my name made it to the cover of one of the Chicken Soup for the Soul books. My largest royalty check was $2.56. Put this venture in the column of less profitable.

Here are a few ideas about how I personally have supported my family over the past twenty years:

- Speaking

- Writing

- Consulting

- Serving as an expert witness in medical malpractice lawsuits

- Serving as a spokesperson for organizations, including a being the health and wellness expert for the largest chain of family-owned pharmacies in the US (hats off to the progressive Bartell Drugs in Washington state) and a national chain of senior-living facilities for which I was the caregiving expert

- Coaching: helping others achieve a desired outcome

- Creating training programs to give family members the tools and skills to make a positive difference for loved ones in pain through their human connection. It's based on a CPR model, with easy instructions to train the trainer and reach many communities.

- Launching into entrepreneurial efforts. I recently cofounded an organization called Beauty Code Genetics. We help women buy the right foundation shade on the basis of a DNA test. My business partner, an organization called Academic Technology Venture, brings the know-how and a process for identifying disruptive academic intellectual property and building and launching companies around them. Right now we're in the proof-of-concept phase.

I decided against what is most likely the most profitable opportunity for a physician leaving clinical medicine: stepping into a leadership role in a healthcare organization, insurance company, or medical device company. While we need good leaders, my career choices have been guided by interest to represent the voice of patients—not stakeholders of companies.

Consider what you really love doing, and find creative ways to do it. I would be happy to spend ten minutes on the phone with you.

Action Steps

- Get a sense of the revenue generated by each of your clinical activities.

- Consider whether you want to focus the scope of your clinical practice.

- If you would like to increase your income, consider other ways to leverage your skills, knowledge, and experience.

MISTAKE #6: FAILURE TO PLAN FOR FINANCIAL MENOPAUSE AND BEYOND

Key Ideas

- Three events have major financial consequences: selling or being bought out of a practice, withdrawing funds in retirement, and dying.
- The best time to plan for these transitions is TODAY.
- Navigating these life events is not a do-it-yourself job; recruit a trusted team.

Gary is a wealth manager who helps many surgeons take control of their financial destiny. One day I asked him, "Why do you work with surgeons?"

He said, "I want to help my surgeon clients avoid the mistakes my own surgeon father made. My dad would give the shirt off his back to a person in need. One day he had to tell me the truth: He had outlived his money. After speaking with my wife, we invited Dad to live with us. I think the injury to his pride killed him."

Transitioning to Retirement: Financial Menopause and Beyond

No matter how much wealth physicians and dentists accumulate, most share a common, deep fear: Will I outlive my money?

I once met a couple in the midst of a crisis. The septic tank in their summer home failed, and the fear in their voices made me wonder if the repair would bankrupt them. Later in the conversation I learned that they built a portfolio worth about $28 million. Yet, the wife was plagued with the fear that she would someday wind up as a homeless bag lady.

You have spent your career building your net worth. During retirement you will shift from the accumulation phase of your financial life to the distribution phase. I call this transition from your productive, earning years to your retirement years "financial menopause."

The rules change when you shift from asset accumulation to asset distribution. This financial stage comes with its own costly mistakes you can avoid.

Three Major Financial Events in Financial Menopause and Beyond

The way you manage these three financial events will contribute significantly to your ability to enjoy your golden years and leave a financial legacy.

- Selling or being bought out of a practice as you enter retirement

- Withdrawing money from your retirement account

- Dying

If you want the transition into retirement to be successful—to trust that the practice you sell will continue to fund your retirement, that you will not outlive your money and that the bulk of your estate will go to your family instead of the IRS—make a plan.

These life transitions elicit strong emotions, and it's easy to let your emotions guide your choices. It may lead to procrastination or denial, which can be a costly mistake.

In this chapter you will find some questions and ideas to bring to your financial dream team as you navigate each life event.

Selling Your Medical or Dental Practice

If you have an ownership stake in your medical or dental practice, you may see your practice as your retirement nest egg. The practice needs to be sold in order to reap the financial rewards of your years of investments.

Here are some costly financial mistakes around the sale of the practice:

Failure to Sell the Practice by Walking Away

Ted looked tanned and rested for the first time in years. I asked him what had changed. He told me, "A few years ago I hit the brick wall; my practice was draining the life from me. I knew I needed out, so I decided to give my practice to my son-in-law."

When I asked him if he had considered selling his practice, he said, "Quite honestly, I didn't have the energy to find a buyer. Sometimes I think about the money I could have gotten had I sold it. Then I tell myself I've just given my daughter an early inheritance."

Before giving away your practice or simply shutting the doors, check with a business appraiser to get a sense of its potential sale value.

Failure to Optimize the Sales Price of Your Practice

You can take steps starting today to optimize the value of your practice.

Failure to Minimize the Taxes You Pay from a Poorly Structured Buy-Sell Agreement

Consider the doctor I know who paid 80% of the sale price of the practice in taxes. Work with the right team who can help you structure the sale in a way that will minimize your tax burdens.

Failure to Make Smart Choices about Your Accounts Receivable

Your receivables are most likely your most valuable practice asset. You have a choice about who owns and collects the accounts receivable that reflect services rendered before the sale.

Failure to Explore a Salary After the Sale

You may want to continue to assure a smooth transition to the new owner. You may not be ready to retire and want to remain on a part-time basis. The buyer will decide whether he or she can afford to keep you on.

Let's move on to the second major financial event you need to plan for: retirement.

Safely Withdrawing Money from Your Retirement Account: The Sequence of Returns

Before retirement, you squirreled away money in different "buckets of bucks"—stocks, bonds, real estate, insurance policies, commodities like gold, equities, or maybe your collection of cars/art/memorabilia.

During your retirement, you will dip into these buckets. How much will you take from each bucket, and in which order?

How will your plans change in a bear market or at times of inflation?

These are the most important questions to ask in retirement to assure you will not outlive your money. The answers will determine how long you can fund your retirement and how much you leave to your heirs.

Ask your wealth manager to do computer modeling and play out different distribution scenarios.

Anticipate your expenses. Will your expenses go up or down in retirement? It depends. Yes, usually the house is paid off and the kids are through college; however, people in retirement generally have a vacation mentality. Get a sense of your average expenditures to fund your desired retirement lifestyle.

Plan for long-term care. David enjoys material abundance, so he is the first person to whom relatives turn in times of need. His mother and two of her sisters were diagnosed with Alzheimer's, and David is paying for the care of all three.

While he wants to help, he knows that the average life expectancy for a patient with Alzheimer's is eight to ten years after the diagnosis, and that memory care can be costly. He worries that the care of his relatives might threaten his own ability to retire one day.

You see from your own clinical experience that people are living longer. Further, life with chronic disease can be costly.

Some questions to consider, include

- What are your parents' plans for long-term care?

- What are your plans for your long-term care?

- What are you doing to remain healthy as you age?

Can You Buy Insurance to Guarantee You Will Not Outlive Your Money?

Yes, you can! You can purchase annuities.

You may have heard that annuities are a "bad investment." Think of annuities as a specific financial tool for a specific job: insuring that you will not outlive your money. This tool is not for everybody.

Further, not all annuities are the same. Do some comparison shopping. Make sure you are getting your advice from a reputable source. Ask lots of questions before you make the purchase.

And now the third major financial event to plan for: your death.

Planning for Your Death

Marie knew that her father had built significant wealth the old-fashioned way—he worked hard, lived well below his means, and saved. He was a simple man who would have preferred to keep his money under his mattress. He had a deep distrust of banks after living through the Great Depression.

Before her father died, he told the kids that his estate would be equally divided among them.

After his death, the family was shocked to see how much of his estate—including his 401(k)—was diverted to pay various tax bills. Marie's own wealth manager said, "It's a shame that your father did not have an estate plan. Had he done so, many of those taxes could have been avoided."

Here are some steps to take to assure that your estate does not lose millions of dollars after your death.

Update your will and insurance beneficiaries. Make sure that your estate is divided in a way that reflects your current relationships. A physician named his wife as the beneficiary when he purchased life insurance. Over the years, he failed to update the name after he divorced and remarried. His widow said, "I was so angry I could kill him!"

Use estate planning financial tools to minimize estate taxes. Work with an estate planner to explore various estate planning tools like living trusts. Explore tools to make charitable contributions or set up your own foundation.

Financial Menopause Need Not Be Feared

Most physicians approach retirement with a mix of joy and fear. Their work with patients has given their life meaning. Most of their socializing may have been with colleagues.

Physicians who thrive in retirement have found ways to engage in activities that bring them joy. Usually that includes serving their families, communities, or causes in some way.

Financial security gives retired physicians freedom to serve in different ways. Maybe it's building a hospital in Africa. Maybe it's writing a memoir. Maybe it's paying for grandkids' college educations. Avoiding financial mistakes allows all of this to happen.

Action Steps

- Create a picture of your ideal retirement lifestyle.
- Calculate your projected yearly income to fund this lifestyle.
- Consider what you can do TODAY to achieve these retirement goals.

PART III
FAILURE TO PLAN
FOR COSTLY AND
IMPROBABLE DISASTERS

We live in a world of risk. And I'm not just talking about lions and tigers and bears. I could tell you stories about ways in which doctors lost their wealth that would curl your toes.

In the next three chapters I discuss three classes of events that could potentially cost you millions of dollars:

- Mistake #7: Losses from theft, fraud, and legal judgments

- Mistake #8: Losses from disability, early death, and natural disasters

- Mistake #9: Losses from investing disasters

These three chapters are not intended to frighten you. The chances of your stepping onto any of these financial landmines are very, very small. The consequences, however, are so potentially devastating that I strongly recommend you consider how you address each risk with your financial dream team and explore ways to protect yourself.

You decrease the damage from these financial traumas the same way you minimize the damage from disease:

- Prevention. You can decrease the risk of any of these disasters happening through awareness and the implementation of policies and procedures.

- Early detection.

- Treatment and recovery. How do you make yourself financially whole if any of these events happen to you?

My intention is not to give you legal or financial advice. You want custom advice that is crafted to meet your needs. You can take these thoughts to members of your financial dream team and explore ways to protect yourself.

MISTAKE #7: FAILURE TO PROTECT YOURSELF FROM BAD PEOPLE

Key Ideas

- As a doctor, you are a target of theft, fraud, and lawsuits.
- You can take steps to prevent losses from known risks.
- Put a barrier around your assets to protect them.

Aaron had done a good job of saving and investing, and at age seventy he continued to work because he enjoyed it.

One day he sent the office manager out to pick up lunch for the team when the unspeakable happened. She was in a car accident in which a teenager was killed. The grieving family hired a lawyer to go after the doctor. Aaron lost everything in a legal judgment against him.

You Are at Risk of Becoming a Victim of Financial Predators

As a doctor, your risk for theft, fraud, and legal judgments is higher than for the average American. Here are the top three reasons why.

Financial predators put Sutton's Law into action. When Willy Sutton was asked, "Why do you rob banks?" he answered, "Because that's where the money is." According to the US Department of Labor Statistics, nine out of the ten top earners in the US call themselves "doctor." This makes you an attractive target for financial predators.

Physicians and dentists tend to be trusting. As a group, doctors want to see the best in others. We're willing to give people the benefit of the doubt—even when the evidence suggests otherwise.

I remember walking across the parking lot from the hospital to my office when a crying woman approached me for some help. She said that her son was just admitted to Children's Hospital, and she didn't have money for gas. Could I help? I felt good about giving her all the cash I was carrying. That is, until the next day when I overheard one doctor say to another, "Can you believe that woman with the gas money scam is back? Does anyone fall for that anymore?"

Physicians and dentists have less financial sophistication than businesspeople. Our business is to take care of patients; taking care of our money usually runs a distant second. Unless we seek it out, we do not have access to the financial tools and skills that help business-minded people protect their wealth and make smart financial choices. This also makes us more vulnerable to financial predators.

You could potentially lose millions of dollars to financial predators that take the form of people looking for investors, employees, and lawyers.

Beware of Financial Predators Asking for Investments

You might have read about the investing fraud perpetrated by John Clark. He told members of his church that he and a business partner belonged to a top-secret US military and government program and held special security clearances that enabled them to invest in the purchase and sale of Iraqi dinar and oil contracts. He promised that $1,000 invested would return $125,000 and a $20,000 investment would guarantee a $3 million payout within ninety days.

According to court documents, Clark himself told investors the returns were "too good to be true" and all they had to do to cash in was to "keep their mouths shut." And forty-seven investors handed over $2 million.

Physicians are targets for predators like John Clark. Here are some warning signs to help you identify them—and avoid becoming their prey:

- **Be wary of get-rich-quick schemes.** If it sounds too good to be true, it usually is.

- **Be wary of no-risk opportunities, guarantees, or promises.** Do you know any medical interventions that have no risk?

- **Be wary of high-pressure sales tactics.** Do not be rushed into a decision.

- **Be wary of a lack of transparency.** Legitimate investment opportunities do not require secrets, stories instead of a prospectus, illegal activities, IOUs, or wiring funds to offshore accounts.

- **Listen to your intuition.** When that still, small voice tells you something is not right, listen!

- **If you have been taken in by a financial predator in the past, know you are not alone.** How did Bernie Madoff steal the life savings of so many smart, successful people? He was a charming sociopath. They can be very difficult to identify. Forgive yourself for past mistakes and move on.

Beware of Financial Predators You May Employ

It had been a while since I saw my colleague Claire at medical meetings. When I asked one of my friends about her, she whispered, "Didn't you hear? Her office manager embezzled her entire retirement. She found out and went into a major depression."

Medical practices have the highest embezzlement rate of any service industry. According to an MGMA study, 83% of medical practices report that they have been victims of embezzlement.

Here are some steps you can take to decrease the risk of theft at home and at your office.

Hire the right people at home and at work. Verify the information provided by the applicant. Call references. Conduct a criminal and credit check for all new employees.

Develop policies, procedures, and protocols. Create a written policy outlining your zero tolerance of fraud and have each employee sign it.

Purchase liability insurance that includes coverage for employee theft and embezzlement. Bond all staff who process payments.

Know the warning signs. Worrisome employee behavior includes

- Spending habits that exceed salaries

- Refusal to take vacations or time off

- Unusual or long work hours

Listen to your gut. If you are worried about an employee, don't dismiss the concern.

Help Keep Honest People Honest

You can remove temptation by keeping items of high value under lock and key. This might mean keeping jewelry in a locked safe at home, securing a lockbox at work, and restricting access to financial records.

Beware of Lawsuits

One physician said, "I feel like I have target on the back of my white coat, and right under it, it says, 'Sue me.'"

Your risk for being sued is higher than for the average American. Here's why:

You engage in high-risk professional activities. Patients consent to medical care knowing that they run the risk of complications and even death. Yet when patients do experience bad medical outcomes, family and friends might encourage them to see a lawyer (who are easy enough to find!).

You work in a highly regulated industry. You run the risk of being investigated and potentially prosecuted for issues related to unprofessional conduct, HIPAA violations, and fraudulent billing practices. As one physician said to me, "When I was investigated for medical fraud, I was assumed guilty until I could prove myself innocent."

People can slip through your danger detector. Whom can you trust and who represents a potential legal and financial threat to you? You run the risk that sociopathic patients, potential employees, financial advisors, and even colleagues can come into your life. Have you known any physicians who have played out their own private version of Fatal Attraction? I have.

After getting sued by a patient, John had his radar up for other patients who might sue him. Yet he was surprised when he learned his trusted nanny was stealing and selling his wife's jewelry.

Your actions have different consequences. Every day thieves steal laptops and smartphones. It's a huge hassle to replace them and try to restore the data. But consider this: What happens if your office manager's laptop is stolen, and she has uploaded medical records that are not encrypted? A physician to whom this happened discovered that he could be liable for a $250,000 fine for each unsecured medical record that was lost.

We live in a litigious society. If someone trips at your house during a Christmas party or your teenager is in a car accident, your risk of being sued is much higher than if you were a teacher.

Lawyers want to try cases with big settlements. Why? Most lawyers decide which cases they take on the basis of their probability of winning—and the number of zeros in the award. Physicians are considered "deep pockets." Lawyers looking for big settlements sue doctors. The more unprotected assets a lawyer can find, the bigger target you are.

Here are some tips to lower your risk of lawsuits.

Create a Fortress around Your Assets

When a lawyer is deciding whether or not to sue you, part of the question is the ease at which the lawyer can capture your assets. You are less attractive to lawyers when a corporate structure—not you—owns your assets. Think of corporation ownership as a moat around your castle.

You can further protect your assets like your accounts receivables or your real estate investments by taking out a small loan on them. Then your lender has a first claim against them in the event of a catastrophic financial judgment.

Place money in buckets that cannot be seized in the event of judgment against you.

Every state has a list of assets or properties that are exempt from seizure. Check with members of your financial dream team to explore whether your retirement account or the cash value of your life insurance policy is protected from creditors.

The best time to make a plan to protect your assets is today.

Get good insurance.

Here are some insurance policies to consider purchasing:

- An umbrella insurance policy for your home (include the rider for identity theft)

- Professional liability insurance

- Disability insurance

- Property insurance for your office

- Business auto insurance

- Business interruption insurance

- Life insurance

- An errors and omissions policy to cover social media activity for your practice

- Practice overhead insurance

- Key employee insurance

- A cyber insurance policy

Action Steps

- Be aware that financial predators exist. And many target physicians and dentists.
- Meet with members of your dream team to assure that you have built a moat around your assets.
- Trust your gut. If you get a funny feeling about an employee or an investment opportunity, listen!

MISTAKE #8: FAILURE TO PLAN FOR DISEASE, UNTIMELY DEATH, AND OTHER DISASTERS

Key Ideas

- Bad things can and do happen.
- The financial consequences of disability, early death, longevity and natural disasters can be astronomical.
- You can purchase many forms of insurance to mitigate against financial losses.

Dana and Paul, married cardiothoracic surgeons, spent Saturday morning squabbling. As Dana saw her husband pull out the ladder to clean the gutters, she said to him, "We have so little time together as a family. Let's just hire someone to clean the gutters, and we can take the kids out to breakfast."

He said, "Give me an hour and it will be done."

She happened to glance out the window to witness her husband reach for a branch that had fallen on the roof, see the ladder slip, and watch her husband fall on the outstretched arm of his dominant hand. After several surgical procedures and multiple rounds of physical therapy, his hand was never the same. He knew that his days operating on the human heart were over.

Bad Things Can and Do Happen

While we would like to believe that we are immune from the trauma and illnesses we see every day with our patients, the reality is that unlikely events touch the lives of doctors too.

I never would have imagined that one day my house would literally go up in smoke, but June 16, 2005, it happened to me when my dryer malfunctioned. I got a firsthand appreciation of the power of preparation and the consequences of working with the wrong people.

I had different insurance companies for my home and car, and both were destroyed. I cannot say enough good things about the compassion and care of the people who helped me replace my home and my possessions. On the other hand, I cannot say enough bad things about my car insurance company. I got the sense that I was the car insurance company's servant rather than customer.

Here are some events I hope never happen to you. But just in case, you can prevent the loss of millions of dollars by preparing for them.

Protect Your Most Precious Asset

Your most valuable asset is not your house or your car collection or your art. Your earning potential is your most valuable asset.

Insure your paycheck. Purchase high-quality same-occupation disability insurance. Period. And hope you never need it.

Protect Your Family If You Die Too Soon

You know from your own clinical experience that some people die well before their time. What would happen to your family if you were to be killed by a drunk driver? Get life insurance.

There are many kinds of life insurance. Speak with someone you trust about what your options are and the kind of life insurance that would help you meet your overall personal and financial goals. These goals change over your life, so revisit this.

Revisit your life insurance needs as your life circumstances change. Your second husband or wife would not be happy to learn that the ex is still listed as the beneficiary.

Life insurance offers more than a death benefit. I was surprised to learn that the wealthy purchase life insurance as a tool to build wealth. Banks purchase life insurance. Warren Buffett owns life insurance. The use of life insurance funded the growth of McDonald's.

Leveraging life insurance to build wealth is like an off-label use of medication.

I'm not here to offer you financial advice. However, after speaking with hundreds of doctors and working with hundreds of wealth managers over the years, here's my take.

First, think of investment vehicles like stocks and bonds and real estate and life insurance as tools. Each does a specific job very well. Each has risks and benefits. You want to work with an advisor who can use all of the tools in the toolbox and knows which ones to use for any specific job.

Second, keep your eye on the prize. What do you care most about—how much you pay in fees, or how much wealth you have in the end?

Third, don't just guess about how investment strategies will play out over time. Have someone run the numbers for you in a computer simulation and see how the portfolios perform under different circumstances. Contact me if you would like the name of someone in your area who can run the numbers for you.

My Choice

Here are the reasons I made the choice to purchase life insurance:

1. **Protection from losses when the market tumbles.** The money you make with a life insurance policy is tied to stock market gains. When the market goes up, you do not experience the full financial benefits; however, I see this as an insurance policy that protects me from losses when the market goes down.

2. **Protection from judgments.** In the event that there is a legal judgment against me, my life insurance policy cannot be taken.

3. **Borrowing from my own policy offers a source of tax-free income in retirement.** While we don't know what will happen to taxes in the future, I suspect they will go up. I would rather pay taxes at a known low tax rate than speculate about what will happen in the future.

4. **My heirs will get tax-free money when I die.**

5. **I can use my policy to fund long-term care.**

The bottom line: I purchased life insurance because I like to remove risk and uncertainty. This is not an investment strategy for everyone. As always, the best way to discern what is best for you is to speak with knowledgeable experts who understand your goals and objectives and have experience with all financial tools.

Living Too Long Can Be Costly

As you well know, people are living longer. And, as you also know, long-term care can be quite costly, especially from chronic progressive illnesses like dementia.

One of the deepest, darkest concerns I hear doctors articulate is the fear of outliving their money.

You want to work with a dream team of financial professionals who can create a plan to maintain your desired lifestyle—no matter how long you live or what your care requirements are.

Further, as you enter retirement, know that the sequence in which you tap into your different classes of assets—we call them your "bucket of bucks"—can make a huge difference. Again, computer modeling can help you play out different scenarios.

Not surprisingly, you can purchase a specialized insurance policy to assure that you will never outlive your money. This class of insurance product is known as an annuity.

You might have heard bad stories about annuities. Not all annuities are the same. I strongly recommend that you work with a financial services professional who can lay out the risks and benefits of different policies so you can make informed choices.

Don't just guess about how investment strategies will play out over time. Have someone run the numbers for you in a computer simulation and see how the portfolios perform under different circumstances. Contact me if you would like the name of someone in your area who can run the numbers for you.

Plan for Acts of God and Unlucky Breaks

I mentioned that I experienced a house fire. Imagine how your life would be disrupted in the event of a natural disaster. Purchase top-quality insurance to protect both your home and your practice.

Back up important records, or store them in the cloud. Walk around your house with a video camera to document what you own. This will help in the event that you must replace these items.

Honor your own risk tolerance. Chances are good that you will enjoy your life without any of these disasters befalling you. But if they do, you will be happy that you prepared for them.

I know from my own personal experience recovering from a house fire that it's better to have insurance and not need it than need it and not have it. Honor your own risk tolerance and decide what's right for you.

Action Steps

■ Be aware that doctors are not immune from untoward events.

■ Meet with members of your dream team to assure that you have adequate insurance protection.

■ Review your current policies to assure that your policies sync with your life stage.

MISTAKE #9: FAILURE TO PROTECT YOURSELF FROM BAD INVESTMENTS

Key Ideas

- Physicians are vulnerable to losses from Dumb Doctor Deals (DDDs).
- Protect yourself from financial predators by spotting common red flags.
- Be an investor—not a speculator. Let a bigger wealth-building plan guide your individual investing choices.

Todd, a fifty-three-year-old financial do-it-yourselfer, felt good about the plan he created to save and invest for retirement. Just to make sure, he decided to meet with a financial advisor to see if he was on track to retire at sixty-two.

He was shocked to hear his "real number"—the amount that the financial advisor projected he would have to have accumulated in order to assure that he would not outlive his money maintaining his lifestyle.

Sure, the advisor told him, he could retire at sixty-two—if he was willing to take the risk of outliving his money, or drastically cut back on his spending.

Todd felt anxious. How could he catch up?

Then he heard one of his colleagues talking in the surgeon's lounge about his new investment—a marijuana farm. He said, "Look. Here's my first dividend check. The projected profits are astronomical!"

Could this be Todd's retirement solution? Todd approached his colleague and asked whether he could buy in. This is how he came to own a 5% equity stake. After six months, as he got his own dividend check, it looked as if he had invested in a gold mine.

He was going all in. First, he invested his kids' college funds. Then he decided to liquidate his stock portfolio and invest that in the farm. A year later, all his retirement savings went up on smoke. The principals of the "investment" were scam artists, and all of Todd's money was gone. The lawyers said there was little chance of recovering any of his investment.

Dumb Doctor Deals Can Be Disastrous

Todd fell into a Dumb Doctor Deal (DDD). I hate to add up how much money I have lost in DDDs. As I look back at these investing disasters, I see the image of lemmings following each other off a cliff.

I lost money when I invested in a business venture recommended by a doctor I trusted. I presumed that his good clinical judgment translated to good investing judgment, and I was wrong.

I lost money investing in businesses of friends I wanted to help, often throwing good money after bad.

Then there was the time I acted on a hot stock tip. A buddy in Seattle told me about "the next Microsoft" founded by a former Microsoft executive. I lost most of that investment, and my only consolation is that even sophisticated investors did not see the accounting shenanigans that spun the company's $300 million loss into a $46 million profit.

One of my friends once said, "I love reading the stock prices in the business section of the paper. It's like visiting the graveyard of my money."

Here is why many physicians and dentists are vulnerable to DDDs:

Poor Financial Literacy. Nowhere in medical school or residency do we learn about how to grow wealth. Every doctor invests in continuing medical education, but few invest in financial literacy. One colleague said, "I don't want to become an investment expert. I found a wealth manager who proved his value over time, and

I defer most investing choices to him. All I really care about is whether I'm on track to retire at sixty and leave a legacy to my family and community."

Poor Vetting. Doctors tend to vet the person bringing them the investment, rather than the investment itself.

More Pitches. Most doctors qualify as accredited investors. This means that they are approached with investing opportunities that are not available to the average American.

The Desire to Help. It can be hard to say no to the friend or relative who is passionate about a business opportunity. Whether they are asking you for an investment or a loan, please go into this with your eyes wide open.

Feeling Desperate. The evolving field of behavioral finance has a simple message: Most investors make common investing errors, and they are most vulnerable to costly mistakes when emotions run high. Ironically, the person who is most vulnerable to poor judgment is the person who is feeling desperate. Maybe they have just lost money in a bad investment. Maybe they see that they are behind financially.

Poorly Calibrated "Trust Meters." Doctors as a group tend to be trusting people. We're more likely to give patients and others the benefit of the doubt. Think about what you do when a patient tells you they dropped their pain medication in the toilet. This trusting nature makes us vulnerable to financial predators and others who do not deserve our trust. On the other side, doctors who have been burned may close themselves off to new people or new ideas. They turn to the people they already know, like, and trust for investing advice—whether or not they're in a position to give trustworthy financial advice.

Acting Like a Speculator Instead of an Investor. A physician with a strategic wealth-building plan knows how individual investments synergistically contribute to the whole. They know when, where, and why they will say yes—and no—to an investing opportunity. In the absence of a bigger map to wealth, making choices about investments is often "ready, fire, aim" instead of "ready, aim, fire."

How Do You Avoid Investing in Disasters?

Think of an investment as a machine that puts your money to work making money.

You may decide to invest your money in

- Stocks and bonds

- Real estate

- Private equity

- Commodities (oil, gold, corn)

- Your practice

- Cash

How do you decide which combination of possible investments is right for you? As with making medical choices, each investment choice involves both risks and benefits. The factors to evaluate are these:

- **Risk.** What are the chances that you will lose your money? One doctor nearing retirement said, "I'm more concerned about the return of my money than the return on my money."

- **ROI (Return on Investment).** What is the projected return on the investment?

- **Growth.** How quickly will you see the ROI? If you are at the early stages of your career, growth might be very important to you. Usually high growth is associated with high risk.

- **Liquidity.** What happens if you need easy access to cash? Many physicians, for example, are house rich and cash poor. There are ways of getting cash in exchange for the equity in your house, but that can take some time. Stocks are more liquid, but if you need money urgently, you run the risk of needing to sell when the market is down.

Here are some tips to help you avoid costly investing disasters.

Know Your Number and Create a Wealth Plan

The single best way to avoid DDDs is to create a master wealth-building plan and follow your progress. That way when opportunities come your way, you can make informed choices.

Consider the answers to these questions in advance:

- What are your overall investing goals? If it's beating the market, I invite you to reconsider. What most doctors really want is the freedom to do what they want to do when they want to do it. Physicians who build wealth generally do it with slow, steady effort.

- What is your overall investment strategy?

- How well is your strategy working for you?

- What specific evidence will help you decide if it's time to make a change?

- What changes in your investment strategies could help you get better results?

- What are your criteria for saying yes to an investment opportunity?

- What are your criteria for saying no to an investment opportunity?

- How are you going to limit the amount of loss in any given investment so it doesn't become catastrophic?

Vet the Investment Opportunity

When someone approaches you with an individual investing opportunity, they will most likely tell you a story. The story could be very compelling. You could be even more persuaded by the trust you have in the person telling the story.

Please look beyond that. Have someone who has expertise in business valuation look through the numbers. Do they make sense? If this person is unsure, get a second opinion.

If you're approached for opportunities like day trading that require that you invest both your time and your money, think very carefully before saying yes. Have clarity about the highest value use of your time.

Remove Emotion

We know that many of our financial choices are driven by emotion, including fear and greed. Create an investing process for yourself that increases the chance that you're making considered investing choices with your cerebral cortex—and not your limbic system.

- **Review your wealth map** and ask yourself whether any specific investment aligns with the bigger plan.

- **Take time** to critically evaluate investing opportunities.

- **Talk it over** with members of your financial dream team. If they raise concerns, listen to them.

- **Decide what level of spending/investing** you will make only after sleeping on it or checking with your partner.

- **Understand that you are vulnerable to investing mistakes after you experience losses.** Making hasty decisions to recover losses usually leads to bad outcomes.

- **Learn from your investing mistakes.** Why do surgical departments have morbidity and mortality conferences? The hope is that every surgeon will learn through the mistakes of others. You, too, can learn through both your own investing mistakes and the mistakes of others.

- **Never worry alone.** If you find that you are losing sleep over finances, get help! Revisit your wealth map. Make sure you're on track. Avoid making any investments when you are anxious. Get to calm first.

Consider What to Say When Family and Friends Ask You to Invest with Them

Ellie's son was brimming with excitement. He had just been to a seminar, learning about how much money he could make becoming a supplement distributor. He wanted in! Would she loan him $20K so he could buy into the business? He promised he would pay her back—with interest.

What would you do if you were Ellie?

These can be tough situations, because now you're making choices about your money and about your relationship with people you love. My guess is that you do not offer medical care to family members and friends. Why? Because these personal relationships can cloud clinical judgment. And these relationships can cloud financial judgment too.

While you will decide what makes the most sense for you when friends and family members ask for loans or investments, here are a few guidelines:

- **Never invest more than you can afford to lose.**

- **Decide what's most important: the relationship or the money.** You could find yourself in a situation in which you lose one or the other—or both—if the investment goes south.

- **If you feel called to help a friend or relative, consider giving them a financial gift.** This approach allows you to maintain the health of the relationship.

- **You always have the option of saying no.** You have neither a moral nor an ethical obligation to fund the investments of friends and relatives. You remember the wisdom of Polonius in Hamlet, "Neither a borrower nor a lender be."

- **Avoid codependent financial rescues.** If you find yourself repeatedly coming to the rescue of a loved one, chances are good that history will keep repeating itself until you do something differently. Sometimes saying no is the most difficult act of love.

Be Guided by Warren Buffett's Two Rules of Investing

Here are Warren Buffett's two rules of investing:

Rule #1: Avoid losses.

Rule #2: Don't forget rule #1.

Minimizing investing disasters is a critical step in your efforts to build wealth.

Action Steps

- Create a wealth-building plan.
- Vet investing opportunities.
- Decide to whom you will give and loan money.

YOUR NEXT STEPS

Congratulations for making this investment in yourself. It takes courage to take an honest look at where you are financially and where you would like to be. However, ideas without action are just hopes and dreams.

Reading this book is just the beginning. Now it's time to take action.

Do you remember the story of the Three Little Pigs? The Big Bad Wolf was coming, and the pigs needed protection. One built a house of straw. A second built a house of twigs. A third built a house of bricks. Each house provided a different level of protection from danger.

What is your current level of protection for each of the money mistakes you want to avoid? Take a red pen and score yourself.

Your Level of Protection from Mistakes: (Check one box for each mistake)	Fortress	Needs Work	Requires Urgent Attention
Plan for the Biology of Behavior			
Plan to Harness the Power of Leverage			
Plan to Manage Taxes			
Plan to Negotiate			
Plan to Optimize Practice Revenue			
Plan for Financial Menopause and Beyond			
Plan for Protection from Bad People			
Plan for Disease, Untimely Death, and Other Disasters			
Plan for Protection from Bad Investments			

Now, Doctor, what is your plan? I invite you to identify a single idea that resonated with you as you were reading. Now translate that idea into action.

My fondest wish for you is that you create the freedom to do what you want to do when you want to do it. That is true wealth.

No matter where you are today, you can make a plan to enjoy a more hopeful tomorrow.

ACKNOWLEDGMENTS

I want to thank the many doctors who have trusted me with their stories of triumphs and struggles.

I also extend my gratitude to the financial advisors in my professional circles who have taught me so much about how money works.

A deep thanks to the people and organizations who invited me to contribute to their publications, speak at their meetings, and appear on their radio shows.

My editor Sandra Wendel always has an intuitive sense of how to communicate ideas clearly. I am eternally grateful for her contributions.

A special thanks to my friends, family, and community who have supported me in a time of transition. My son, Meir, continues to be my eternal source of joy and inspiration.

ABOUT THE AUTHOR

Vicki Rackner, MD, FACS, calls on her thirty-plus-year medical career as a practicing surgeon, as clinical faculty at the University of Washington School of Medicine, and serial entrepreneur to help her doctor clients achieve the personal, professional and financial rewards that attracted them to a career in medicine through her company www.ThrivingDoctors.com.

As a nationally noted author, speaker, and consultant, Dr. Vicki builds the bridge between the world of business and the world of medicine. She's the expert quoted in publications ranging from the Wall Street Journal and Washington Post to Physician's Money Digest to name a few. She is the author of multiple books, including *The Myth of the Rich Doctor, Caregiving Without Regrets*, and *How Doctors Build TrueWealth*.

CNN Senior Medical Correspondent Elizabeth Cohen says, "Don't miss Dr. Vicki Rackner."